I'm Growing!

by Aliki

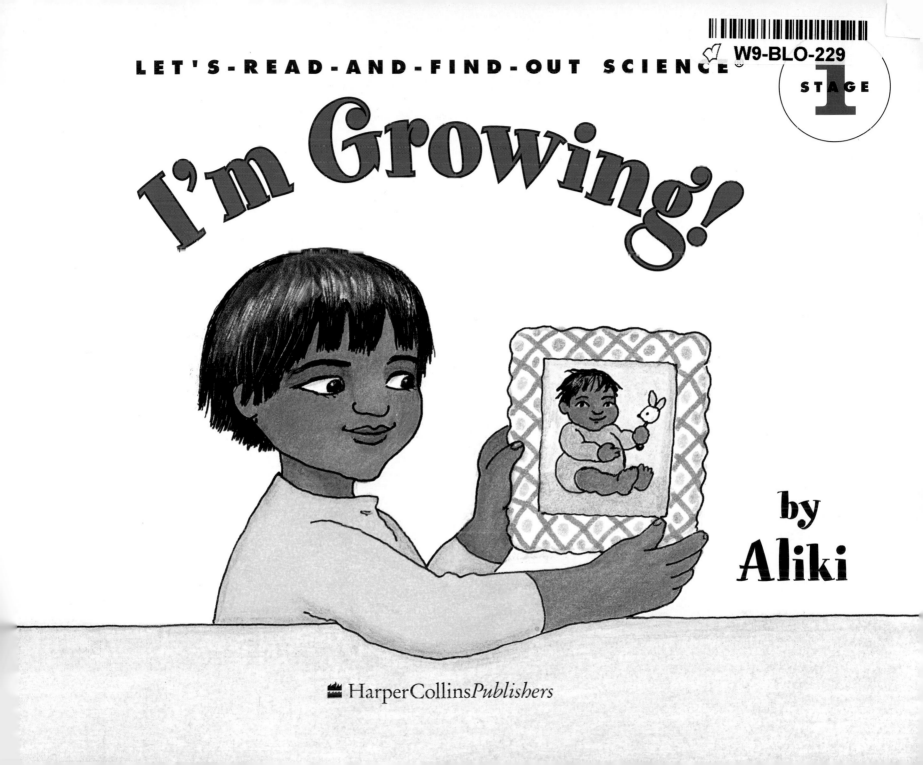

HarperCollinsPublishers

For the growing cousins
Alene, Jim, and Eleanor Rhea
Madeline, Phoebe, and Grace MacCurrah

♥

and for
David, Faviola, and Eric Lomale

The *Let's-Read-and-Find-Out Science* book series was originated by Dr. Franklyn M. Branley, Astronomer Emeritus and former Chairman of the American Museum—Hayden Planetarium, and was formerly co-edited by him and Dr. Roma Gans, Professor Emeritus of Childhood Education, Teachers College, Columbia University. Text and illustrations for each of the books in the series are checked for accuracy by an expert in the relevant field. For more information about Let's-Read-and-Find-Out Science books, write to HarperCollins Children's Books, 1350 Avenue of the Americas, New York, NY 10019, or visit our website at www.letsreadandfindout.com.

I'M GROWING!
Copyright © 1992 by Aliki Brandenberg
Manufactured in Mexico All rights reserved.
ISBN 0-06-445116-X (pbk.)

Look at me!
My clothes don't fit.
My shirt won't button.
My jeans are too short.
The waist doesn't snap.
My shoes are too tight.
My cap won't go on.

I'm growing!

I have been growing for a long time.
Here is a picture of me when I was a baby.
I can't believe how little I was!

Look how I've grown

and grown

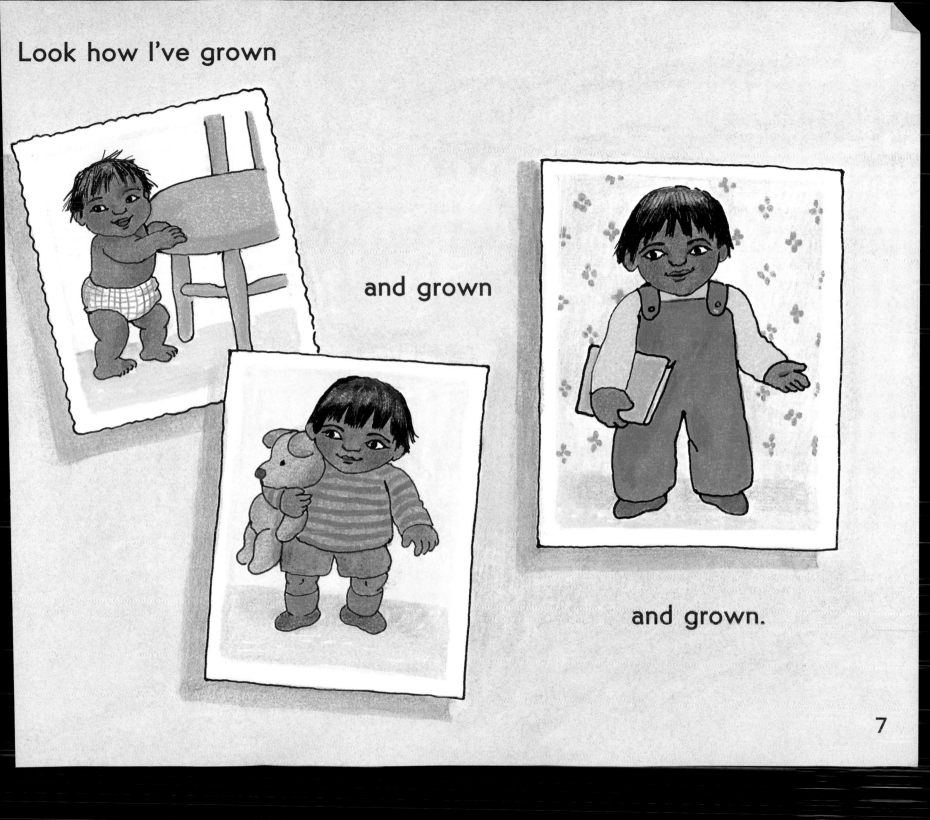

and grown.

I look different now.
The features of my face have changed.
They are bigger—especially my nose.

My arms and legs are longer.
So are my body and my neck.
I am heavier and taller.

While I have been growing on the outside,
I've been growing inside, too.
My bones are bigger.
My muscles are bigger.

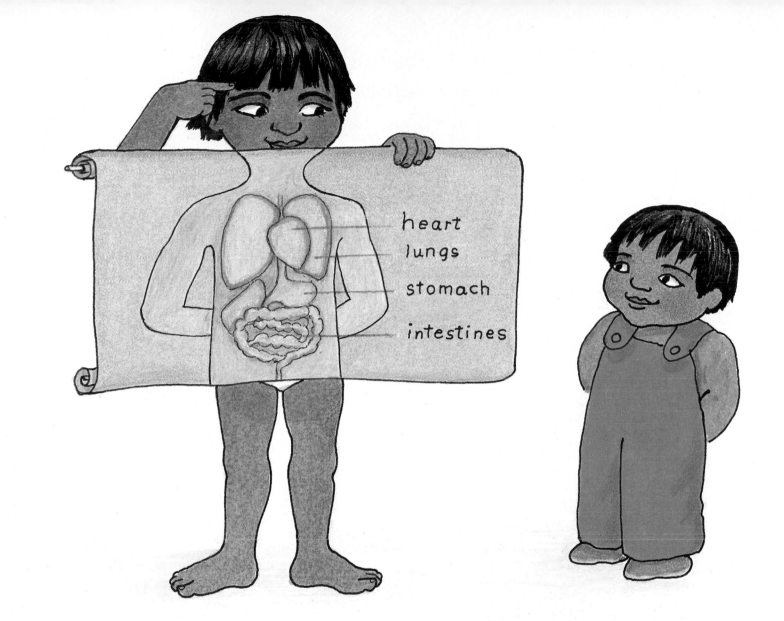

o are my brain, my heart, my lungs, my stomach, and my other organs.

And while everything inside me grows,
the skin that covers me grows, too.
No matter how big your bones get,
your skin will always fit.
You may pop your buttons,
but you can't pop your skin!

When I was a baby, I had baby teeth.
Now I am losing my baby teeth.
My new teeth are bigger.
They will fit my growing face.

I have to take care of my new teeth.
They have to last me all my life.

Most people grow until they reach a certain age.
But sometimes, something goes wrong.
For some reason, a person may grow very little,
or stop growing too soon.
That's what happened to our friend.
He remained small even though he is a grown-up.

Most people stop growing in their late teens.
After that, a person may grow thinner or fatter.

And everyone grows older.
But bones and organs don't grow bigger anymore.

Yet some parts of you don't stop growing.
Hair is always growing.
Look at Anna's.
Anna has never cut her hair.
She can almost sit on it.

Louie's hair grows fast.
He gets a haircut every month.

Jenny's grandfather has lost the hair
on top of his head.
But it keeps growing around the sides.

Fingernails and toenails
never stop growing, either.

When you play, you use up energy.
When you grow, you use up energy, too.
That's why you get hungry.

Food—especially good food, with proteins
and vitamins and minerals in it—
gives you energy.
It helps you grow.

I eat a good breakfast and a good lunch.
When I come home from school, I'm hungry again.
I have a snack.
Then I have a good dinner.
I tell my mother I'm a growing boy.

Not everyone eats the same amount.
Right now I eat more than my big sister
or my little brother.
But they are growing, too.

Not everyone grows at the same time, either.
Some people grow in spurts.
I took a picture with my friends last year.
Look at us now.
Our sizes have changed.
Yet we are all the same age.

We are all growing in our own way,
at our own speed.
When we are all grown up,
we may be the same size.

Or we may end up different sizes.

Right now I am my size, and I am going
to try on my new clothes.

They are a little big, but I'll grow into them.

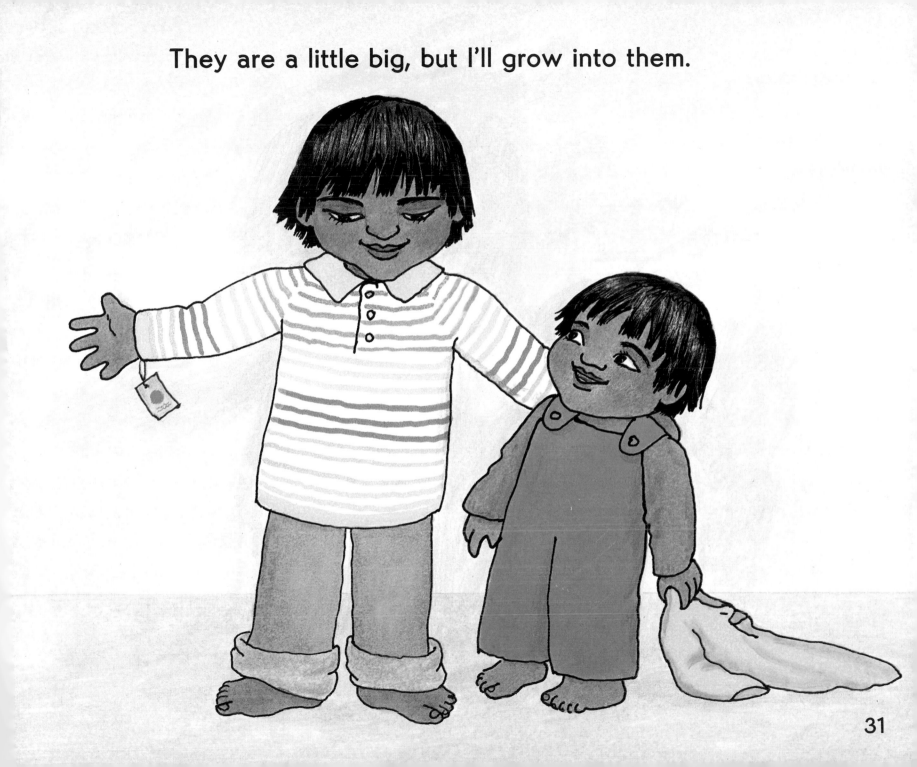

It will happen to you, too.

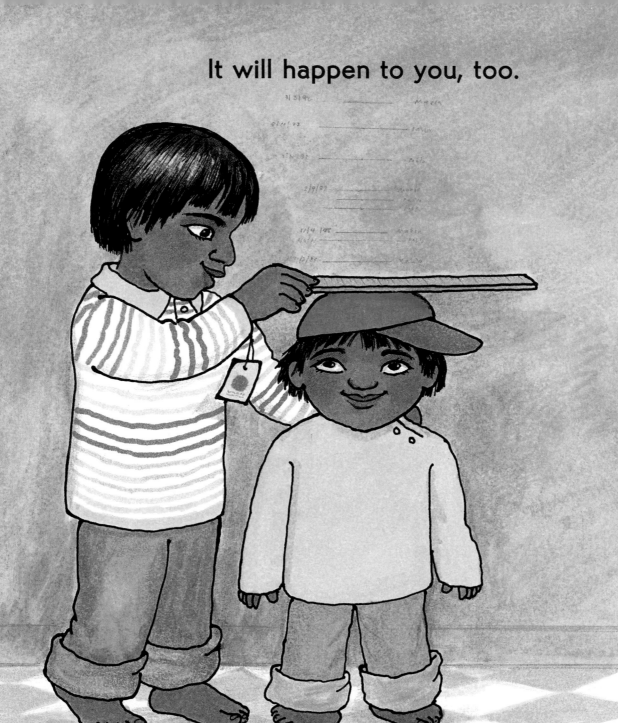